Leoš Janáček
Jenůfa
Její pastorkyňa
IHRE ZIEHTOCHTER

Universal-Edition
№ 5821

Cover of the 1917 edition:
"Leoš Janáček. Jenůfa / Her Stepdaughter [or: Foster Daughter]"
The drawing depicts Gabriela Horvátová as the sextoness in the Prague production.

JENŮFA

Vocal Score

Leoš Janáček

DOVER PUBLICATIONS, INC.
Mineola, New York

Bibliographical Note

This Dover edition, first published in 2002, is an unabridged republication of *Jenůfa/Její Pastorkyňa (Ihre Ziehtochter),* the vocal score of the opera in three acts after the drama of Moravian peasant life by Gabriela Preissová. Music by Leoš Janáček. German translation by Max Brod. Piano reduction by Josef von Wöss. Originally published by Universal-Edition, Vienna, 1917.

The introduction and synopsis of the opera were specially prepared for this Dover edition by Stanley Appelbaum, who also provided the following prefatory sections: an English translation of the original credits; the annotated list of characters; a "Buryja Family Tree"; an explanation of instrument abbreviations in the vocal score; and a translation of the Czech texts of the original pictorial cover and of the original title page.

International Standard Book Number: 0-486-42433-2

Manufactured in the United States of America
Dover Publications, Inc., 31 East 2nd Street, Mineola, N.Y. 11501

JENŮFA

Her Stepdaughter

[or: Foster Daughter]

Opera in three acts
after the drama of Moravian peasant life
by Gabriela Preissová

Music composed by

Leoš Janáček

German translation by Max Brod.
(The text was later arranged by Hugo Reichenberger
for a production by the Vienna Imperial Opera.)

Piano reduction with text by Josef V. von Wöss.

Composition and First Performances

Jenůfa was begun in 1894. Act I was completed in 1897;
Act II, in summer 1902; Act III, in March 1903.

The world premiere took place on 21 January 1904,
in Brno, at the theater Na Veveří.

The first performance at the National Theater in Prague was on 26 May 1916.

Act I takes place at the Buryja mill; Acts II and III, in the sextoness' cottage.
Six months elapse between Acts I and II; two months, between Acts II and III.

CHARACTERS

Old lady[1] Buryjovka, retired owner of, and housekeeper, in the mill . . . . . Alto
Sextoness[2] Buryjovka, a widow, daughter-in-law of the old lady . . . . Soprano
Jenůfa, her [the sextoness'] stepdaughter [and foster daughter] . . . . Soprano
Laca Klemeň ⎫ stepbrothers, grandsons of old Buryjovka . . . . Tenor
Števa Buryja ⎭ . . . . Tenor
Foreman[3] of the mill . . . . Baritone
Mayor [and judge] of the village . . . . Bass

Mayor's wife . . . . Mezzo-soprano
Karolka, their daughter . . . . Mezzo-soprano
A shepherdess[4] . . . . Mezzo-soprano
Barena, a servant girl in the mill . . . . Soprano
Jano, a shepherd boy . . . . Soprano

A village woman[5] . . . . Alto
[Another village woman (offstage voice, page 215) . . . . Soprano]
[A village man (offstage voice, page 215) . . . . Baritone]

[Onstage] musicians, villagers. [The chorus also specifically represents
recruits, mill workers, and wedding guests.]

---

[1]"Little old lady" (in Brod's German, *Alte* or *Mütterchen*) is how Jenůfa's grandmother is referred to in the opera (standard Czech, at least, has specific words for "grandmother"). "Grandmother" will be used for clarity in the new front matter of this Dover edition.

[2]Brod's German translation is *Küsterin,* a German equivalent of the character's Czech designation *kostelnička* (an endearing diminutive of *kostelnica*), of which "female sexton" or "sextoness" is the exact English counterpart. This is the character's title of respect, not her proper name; and, though it is obviously handy to retain "Kostelnicka" [*sic*] in an English singing (or other) translation, it is nevertheless just as absurd as it would be to call the Queen of the Night "Königin" in an English-language *Magic Flute.* In the new Introduction and Synopsis she will be called the sextoness or merely Jenůfa's stepmother.

[3]Often mistranslated as "miller" or "old man."

[4]"Shepherdess" is the normal meaning, but the character is often called "a maid" in both German and English renderings. It has also been suggested that she is an inmate of the village poorhouse.

[5]This character, who sings a few words in the climactic Act Three ensemble, is called *tetka* (literally, "aunt") in the original, and has been called "aunt" in some German and English renderings, though no relationship to any other character is established. This "aunt" may be simply a term of endearment for a mature village woman.

Buryja Family Tree

[The following family tree and description of the characters, the latter using scattered clues in the libretto and in parts of the original play that Janáček jettisoned, are new additions to this Dover edition.]

The people in lower case are already deceased when the opera begins; the people in small capitals are actual characters in the opera. Generations align horizontally (the youngest generation decreases in age from left to right). Double lines indicate marriages; single lines indicate offspring of those marriages. The numbers indicate the sequence of marriages for the two people who remarried: Laca's mother and Jenůfa's father.

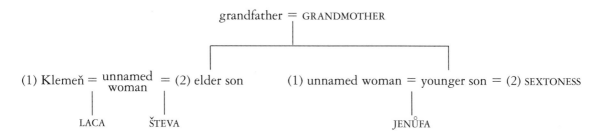

The grandmother inherited the mill (and the sizeable farmland attached to it) from her husband, but made it over to her elder son, on whose death the ownership passed to Števa, though his grandmother reserved an annuity (or a share) for her old age, and she continues to live in the mill, serving as chief housekeeper.

That elder son married the widow of a man surnamed Klemeň, who already had a son, Laca (short for Ladislav), from her own first marriage. The offspring of the new marriage was Števa (short for Štefan) Buryja, four years younger than Laca. Števa now owns the mill, while Laca is merely kept on as a journeyman miller. Since Števa is just now eligible for conscription into the army, both stepbrothers are still young. Laca, long in love with Jenůfa, has already put in three years' army service; when he got home, he found Jenůfa deeply involved with Števa.

Jenůfa (Genevieve; three years younger than Števa) was the only child of Grandmother Buryjovka's younger son. Her mother died while she was still an infant, and her father (now dead) married the woman known as the sextoness, who lovingly raised Jenůfa as if she were her biological daughter. The sextoness actually does perform a sexton's duties in the village chapel (plot summaries that call her a sexton's wife are absolutely incorrect). An educated woman who has educated Jenůfa as well, she is highly respected in the village. Jenůfa is currently living at the mill, where she helps with the household chores; her actual domicile is the sextoness' cottage.

Introduction to the Dover Edition

Opera was the central genre in the varied oeuvre of Leoš Janáček (1854–1928). He started to sketch out operas in 1885, and he wrote his first one, *Šárka,* in 1887 (revised several times before its first performance in 1925 in Brno, the chief city of the composer's native Moravia, and his home since 1880).[1] Untypically for Janáček, *Šárka* was a Late Romantic opera based on legendary Czech history. His second opera, *Počátek románu* (Beginning of a Romance), was written in 1891 and first performed in Brno in 1894; it has a village milieu, but the folk spirit is rather artificial, though the composer makes extensive use of folksong and folkdance. His third opera, *Jenůfa,* his first great one, and still the favorite of some listeners and critics, was to be his—slowly achieved—breakthrough to fame beyond his native region.

In the years before its composition, he had been collecting Moravian folk music in the field (he began in 1888, six years before Bartók was to do the same in Hungary; but Janáček had already become enchanted with rural Moravia during summer travels in 1875), he had made arrangements of numerous folksongs, he had composed many choral works (some of them narrative in nature, with a textual and musical bearing on the future *Jenůfa*), and he had been evolving his very personal compositional method of speech-melody, based on the lilt of actual speech.

In the play from which he derived *Jenůfa,* he at least found an ideal opera subject. Many of the themes that were to obsess him all his life—lovers' jealousy, a central character's isolation from his community, violence and death with subsequent forgiveness and renewal of life on a higher plane—all these were present, and acted out on his own native soil.

Source and Libretto. This play, *Její pastorkyňa,*[2] was written by Gabriela Preissová,[3] who had already been associated with Janáček, since his second opera had been based on one of her short stories. Preissová (1862–1946) was from Bohemia, but when she married in 1880 she went to live in Slovácko, a rural district of Moravia with a heavy Slovakian tinge. She absorbed the local customs and dialect, and used them extensively in her writings. She wrote stories, novels, opera librettos (some for Smetana), and plays that inspired yet further operas. Her plays, especially, influenced by Russian naturalism and daring for their time, broke away from the Romantic and Neoclassical veins then still current in Bohemia and Moravia; they often concern star-crossed lovers. *Její pastorkyňa* created such a furor that it was withdrawn after only five performances, discouraging its author from pursuing her revolutionary writing campaign. (She later wrote a short novel of the same name, greatly expanding the plot backward in time; *Její pastorkyňa* was filmed in Czechoslovakia in 1929 and 1938.)

The play, based on two real-life incidents, was first performed in Prague on November 9, 1890, and was published in 1891 by F. Šimáček in Prague as No. XXIV in the series "Repertoir Českých Divadel" (Repertoire of Czech Theaters). Janáček could have seen it when it was performed in Brno in 1891. At any rate, he contacted the playwright by 1893 about the possibility of making an opera out of it; she was reluctant at first, not believing it would work, but Janáček began his own adaptation of the play into a libretto in 1894.

Changing only a few words, he retained the original structure and dialogue, but he made countless small cuts, and a few big ones, in order to leave more time for music. Some of his cuts in the text were very effective, especially at the very end of each act, where his greater concision is highly dramatic; but many of his other cuts have left the libretto somewhat incoherent with regard to the characters' relationships, place of residence, more specific motivations, and the like (the notes to the Synopsis and to the list of characters in this volume restore some of this information). In general, whenever adapting a libretto from a literary source, Janáček was apparently unconcerned about incoherency, relying on his music to either flesh out the situations or at least distract the listener.

A distinctive feature of the resulting libretto is that it is in prose, still a great novelty at the time. Some of Mussorgsky's *Boris Godunov* (1869, 1874) is in prose, but that opera was not yet well known outside of Russia. The only examples of prose librettos apparently known to Janáček were those to the French operas of Alfred Bruneau (1857–1934). When Janáček adapted Preissová's play, such outstanding examples of prose librettos as those for Charpentier's *Louise* (1900), Debussy's *Pelléas et Mélisande* (1902), and Strauss's *Salome* (1905) were still in the future. On the other hand, in *Jenůfa* the regular flow of the prose is counteracted by an unusually great number of word repetitions, introduced by the composer, which to some extent reinstate a verselike feeling.[4]

The play and libretto are extensively in regional dialect, affecting not only word forms, but much of the vocabulary, which differs from standard Czech and includes a large number of German loanwords (there were historical reasons for this strong German influence in the area). In the three folksongs (the recruits' song, the song called "Jenůfa's favorite," and the bridesmaids' song) the dialect is even further from standard Czech, closer to pure Slovakian.[5] Jenůfa and her stepmother, more educated, speak dialogue that is more like standard Czech.

Composition and Premiere. *Jenůfa* had a long gestation period. It was begun in 1894, but the first act was only completed in 1897 (Janáček composed directly in full score, via sketches). Then he became busy with other projects (he had a heavy teaching schedule, conducted choirs, etc.), and apparently he was rethinking his compositional methods. He returned to work on *Jenůfa* in late 1901, and completed the second act during the summer of 1902. The third act was done by March 1903 at the latest. The last phase of composition was saddened by the illness of his daughter Olga (1882–1903), who had caught typhoid fever on a trip to Russia. (Janáček's second child, Vladimir, had died of meningitis, at age two, in 1890.)

On completion of the opera, Janáček had his heart set on a more prestigious world premiere in Prague, and he sent a copy to the composer and conductor Karel Kovařovic (1862–1920), chief conductor of opera at the National Theater from 1900 until his death. Kovařovic rejected the manuscript, alleging among other reasons its crude orchestration and its annoying word repetitions. From that day to this, many people believe that this rejection was a personal vendetta for Janáček's scathingly sarcastic review of one of the conductor's operas in 1887.

The premiere took place in Brno, at the theater called Na Veveří, on January 21, 1904; it was conducted by a pupil of the composer's, the highly competent Cyril Metoděj Hrazdira (1868–1926).[6] It was a great local success, even though the orchestra didn't include every instrument that the score calls for. (There were numerous performances in Brno that year, and there were new Brno productions in 1906, 1911, and 1913, Janáček making some revisions all the time—particularly in 1906/07—sometimes in response to specific suggestions by Hrazdira.)

Meanwhile, in December 1904, Janáček contacted Mahler, who had been conducting at the Vienna Imperial Opera (Hofoper) since 1897; a production (in German) at the capital of the empire might catapult his work into Germany and beyond, as had been the case notably with Smetana's *Bartered Bride*. This approach foundered when Mahler asked for a German-language vocal score, something that didn't exist for another thirteen years. Meanwhile, Janáček continued to exert pressure on Kovařovic, who may have attended a performance in Brno in December 1904, but to no avail.

Later Productions. The pressure on Kovařovic mounted over the years, especially when a soprano who was a friend of both composers entered the picture, hoping to sing the role of Jenůfa in Prague; she eventually brought about a reconciliation between them—and then Janáček made no appreciable effort to support her when the role was assigned to someone else! The opera was accepted for Prague late in 1915, with the proviso that Kovařovic could make the revisions he deemed essential for his more cosmopolitan audience. These changes involved a number of cuts (the verbal text was left virtually intact) and an extensive overhauling of the orchestration; Kovařovic donated his fee for the revisions (paid by the Viennese publishing house Universal-Edition, which had agreed to publish the score) to a musicians' charitable fund, and refrained from taking any credit in the score. Janáček apparently consented to the alterations, and may have even participated in them. The Kovařovic, or Prague, version of the score became the standard performing version everywhere for decades to come, and was still the preferred version in Prague in the second half of the twentieth century (more of this below, in the section "The Music").

Kovařovic, a truly fine conductor, held plenty of rehearsals, during which parts of the opera ran afoul of the imperial censors. Jenůfa's prayer to the Virgin in Act Two was finally allowed to remain, but the words of the recruits' song in Act One had to be altered (reluctance to serve in the army was a highly unpatriotic theme while World War I was raging). The Prague premiere, on May 26, 1916, was a decided success, and the unhappily married Janáček had an affair with the Croatian soprano Gabriela Horvátová, who sang the role of the stepmother.

A Viennese production was now a distinct possibility, but for that a German text was needed. Janáček requested this translation of Max Brod, who had heard the opera in November 1916 and had written a warm review. Brod (1884–1968), a pianist, song composer, music and theater critic, and writer of fiction, was a member of the Jewish German cultural community in Prague that also included Franz Werfel and Franz Kafka (as Kafka's literary executor, Brod salvaged most of his works for posterity); later he wrote the first biography of Janáček, and he also translated the librettos of the composer's operas *Kát'a Kabanová, The Cunning Little Vixen,* and *The Makropoulos Affair.* Brod translated *Jenůfa* in 1917, and his version continues to appear in every Universal edition, as well as being the version used when the opera is performed in German.[7] Hugo Reichenberger (1873–1938), who was to be the conductor in Vienna, thought that the Tyrolean dialect of German would be the proper equivalent of the opera's Moravian text; though Brod refused to change his translation, a Tyrolean flavor was used in the Vienna production, and Reichenberger took a credit in the 1917 Universal score, in which the German differs in small details from later editions.

The Vienna premiere, on February 16, 1918, featured the glamorous Maria Jeritza (1887–1982) as Jenůfa (Janáček said she was the best he had heard; the Brno-born soprano had been with the Hofoper since 1913). The composer, who placed great store on production values, was also overjoyed at the sets and folk costumes. An upsurge in his creativity, further sparked by the creation of an independent Czechoslovakia later that year, ensued.

As hoped, the Vienna success opened the operatic floodgates. Before the year was over, Klemperer conducted the work in Cologne. The most important European premiere after Vienna, however, was the one at the Berlin Staatsoper in 1924, conducted by the great Erich Kleiber (1890–1956), who had been named chief conductor of that house the year before, almost immediately after his conducting debut in Berlin. Jenůfa was sung by the Russian soprano Zinaida Jurjewskaja (1896?–1925), then at the midpoint of her meteoric three-year career at the house.[8] Also in 1924, *Jenůfa* was first performed at the Met, with Jeritza as Jenůfa and Margarete Matzenauer as her stepmother; Artur Bodansky conducted. By 1926, *Jenůfa* had been produced at more than 70 opera houses.

Unknown to Janáček, Universal-Edition had paid a one-percent royalty to Kovařovic for his revisions, and after his death in 1920 had continued to pay it to his widow. In 1923, in an economy measure, they ceased doing so, and she dunned the composer for the money, threatening to ban performances of her husband's (universally used) version. In the ensuing wrangle, in which Janáček proposed a similar ban, he repudiated Kovařovic's contributions, insinuating that he had made all the cuts and changes merely to justify his decade-long refusal to mount the opera. After arbitration, Janáček was absolved of the responsibility to pay the royalty (Universal resumed payments), but a legal decision in 1964 found that Kovařovic had truly been an artistic collaborator in the opera. (More about Kovařovic's version in the next section.)

The Music. Janáček is now generally considered as one of the truly inventive geniuses in opera history, and *Jenůfa* is seen as the consolidation of his mature style.[9] It has been called his most intense and concentrated opera, his most Moravian opera, and a minor-key Moravian counterpart to Smetana's buoyant Bohemian *Bartered Bride* (1866). Unlike Smetana and Dvořák, however, Janáček did not strive for an accommodation with Western European, especially German, music; nor did he assign the orchestra a preponderant role in interpreting the action, like Wagner. Yet the influence of all these predecessors can be detected in *Jenůfa,* as well as that of Tchaikovsky, particularly *The Queen of Spades* (1890).

Among Janáček's musical characteristics in *Jenůfa* are: his preference for high voices and tessituras and extreme orchestral registers; the unimportance of counterpoint; the replacement of classical symphonic development by varied repetitions of brief speech-melody patterns; the very restricted use of leitmotifs running through the entire work (instead, he uses so-called situation-motifs within a given scene); a decided folk flavor without the adoption of actual folk tunes (except to some extent in the folksong scenes); a steady musical flow with generally unresolved chords (when a perfect cadence appears, it is effective); the occasional use of church modes and the fleeting occurrence of the whole-tone scale (not employed systematically); and a clean, sometimes sparse ("selective") orchestration, including such effects as the xylophone's imitation of the mill wheel as a sign of inexorable fate. His personal intensity and inventiveness save the music from seeming shortwinded or thin. Act One, which was completed some years before the rest, still shows many traces of being a "number" opera; the other acts are more through-composed. Lastly, *Jenůfa* still contains more vocal ensembles than the later operas, in which

Janáček felt that ensembles robbed him of his opportunity to plumb individual psychology. A useful long description of the music in *Jenůfa* (not precisely an analysis) may be found in Michael Ewans' *Janáček's Tragic Operas* (Indiana University Press, Bloomington, 1977).

Several of Janáček's compositions of the 1890s foreshadow *Jenůfa* in different ways. His 1891 *Suite for Orchestra,* Op. 3 (not performed until 1928, in Brno), contains the tune that has been labeled the "guilt motif" in *Jenůfa* (a clear occurrence is the music to Jenůfa's words "Duša moja, Števo, Števuško" (page 46). The 1892 piano piece "Ej danaj" uses the melody of the wild *odzemek* dance in Act One. From the same year, the work for mixed chorus and orchestra "Zelené sem sela" (I Sowed Green) is similar to the music for the song "Far and Wide" sung in Jenůfa's honor in the same act. In 1893 the male chorus "Vínek" (The Garland) concerns a young man who wishes to pay off the girl he has wronged rather than marry her. In 1894 Janáček wrote an overture for *Jenůfa* expressive of Laca's jealousy; the piece, apparently never performed with the opera, became the separate orchestral work "Žárlivost" (Jealousy).[10]

Controversy continued to rage during the period of *Jenůfa's* world triumph over Kovařovic's revisions. Some very serious and sane commentators approved of everything the Prague conductor had done, both ethically and musically; and it is possible that the opera's path would have been even less smooth in Janáček's pristine version. Kovařovic's version was used by the conductor Jaroslav Vogel (1894–1970; also Janáček's foremost biographer) in the first complete recording of the opera (Supraphon, 1952). The 1969 recording (EMI /Supraphon) by Bohumil Gregor (born 1926), who conducted the opera in San Francisco in that year, departs from Kovařovic only slightly.[11]

Yet champions of Janáček's unaltered original (sometimes hard to determine because the manuscripts are so sloppy) were beginning to make themselves heard. In 1941 Brno Radio broadcast excerpts of a restored version. Finally in 1982 (British) Decca released a thoroughly "cleansed" complete recording conducted by Sir Charles Mackerras (born 1925), a conducting pupil of Václav Talich and long a lover of Czech music. (Nevertheless, even Mackerras, in his remarks in the booklet to his 1976 recording of *Kát'a Kabanová,* admits that the miracles of studio engineering can make acceptable orchestrations that might not work in an opera house.) The general tendency today is to return to Janáček's original in performance; this is in line with the rehabilitation of *Boris Godunov* and Bruckner's symphonies, to cite only two outstanding examples. The proponents of the "cleansing" of *Jenůfa* point out that the opera now features more abrupt orchestral contrasts, revealing that it already forecast similar contrasts familiar from Janáček's late operas, which no Kovařovic ever tempered with.

Publication History. The first complete manuscript of *Jenůfa* burned in 1910. The extensive extant materials on which to base editions are preserved in the Janáček Archive of the Moravian Regional Museum in Brno.

The first vocal score, in Czech only, was published by the Klub Přátel Umění (Friends of Art Club) in Brno in 1908 in an edition of 600 copies, half of which were for club members. The rights to this vocal score were later acquired by the firm Hudební Matice in Prague, but their editions reflected Kovařovic's cuts. Hudební Matice issued several editions, some newly edited, over the decades.

After Richard Strauss heard *Jenůfa* in Prague, he recommended it to Universal-Edition in Vienna, and an Universal representative went to hear it in March 1917, to his satisfaction. In December of that year, Universal issued its vocal score (reprinted in this Dover volume), in a piano reduction by Josef V. von Wöss said to be much better than its 1908 Brno counterpart (which had probably been done by the composer). This 1917 vocal score reflected Kovařovic's cuts, and was the first to include Brod's German translation as well as the original text (the German comes first, and is in Roman, which is clearer than the italic used for the Czech). The first full score of the opera was published by Universal in 1918.

In 1969 Universal issued a full score and a vocal score edited by J. M. Dürr (the first page of music bears a 1967 copyright for the new editing). Substantially adhering to the Kovařovic version, the Dürr edition was the first to include the stepmother's passage in Act One beginning "Aji on byl zlatohřivý" (see note 11 to the Synopsis!), which Janáček had cut on his own, at least before the 1908 vocal score (it may never have been actually performed even before then). Dürr's full score also included, for the first time, English words beneath the German and Czech; the translation was that prepared by Otakar Kraus and Edward Downes for the first performance of *Jenůfa* at Covent Garden in 1956. This English translation is gratifyingly accurate, but very stiff; for example, the endlessly repeated line in Act One (see Synopsis!) that literally means "Every couple must undergo its own suffering" emerges as "Love must always endeavour o'er misfortunes to triumph."

In 1982 Mackerras' recording, undoing Kovařovic's "mischief," was issued, but it took some time for a printed score to reflect this "cleansed" version. In 1991, such a score became available for hire only; but a few years later (1996, according to the New York Public Library catalogue; the score itself merely bears a 1993 copyright on the first music page) Universal-Edition published a full score (the NYPL copy is a miniature score with extremely tiny notes) edited by Mackerras and by John Tyrrell.[12] This score contains the same three languages as the Dürr edition; it made extensive use of old orchestral parts preserved in Brno.

The Present Edition. Since the 1917 Universal vocal score that Dover wished to reprint was entirely in Czech and German, the firm commissioned this Introduction and the Synopsis that follows (the only source of much enlightening information derived from Preissová's original play). Also new to this Dover edition are the family tree and notes following the list of characters, and the note on instrumentation. The original front matter is newly translated.

The 1917 edition does not include the stepmother's additional passage in Act One, but it is described in the Synopsis. Since Kovařovic's revisions, reflected in this 1917 score, chiefly affected the orchestration, and his small cuts were generally in instrumental passages, this vocal score is of the greatest use even to vocal performers of, and listeners to, the Mackerras–Tyrrell version, besides reflecting exactly the way *Jenůfa* has been produced for most of its long international career.

STANLEY APPELBAUM

[1]Up to 1918, Moravia was a separate constituent of the Austro-Hungarian Empire, ruled from Vienna. In 1918 it joined with its neighbor to the west, Bohemia, and its neighbor to the east, Slovakia, to form Czechoslovakia. Since 1993, the former Bohemia and Moravia, together, have constituted the Czech Republic; and the former Slovakia, the Slovak Republic. The national language of the Slovak Republic is Slovakian, a Western Slavic language very closely related to Czech, the language of the Czech Republic. In Janáček's day, probably more than now, Moravia was a cultural bridge between westward-looking Bohemia and eastward-looking Slovakia, and its local dialects were tinged with Slovakian to a greater or lesser degree. (Janáček first left his Moravian village for Brno at age eleven, but only actually settled down there in 1880.)

[2]This can mean either "Her Stepdaughter" or "Her Foster Daughter"; Janáček himself seems to have preferred the former, since he asked for *Stieftochter* as the German equivalent rather than the *Ziehtochter* (a variant of *Pflegetochter*) which Universal-Edition nevertheless adopted in its 1917 vocal score (reprinted in this Dover volume). Either rendering fits the situation of the opera's plot: the sextoness was the second wife of Jenůfa's father, but she raised her from infancy as her own daughter. *Její pastorkyňa* has always been the title of the opera in what is now the Czech and Slovak Republics, but the opera is called *Jenůfa* everywhere else. (The standard Czech form of *pastorkyňa* is *pastorkyně*.)

[3]The -*ová* suffix of a woman's surname (there are other such suffixes, too) is added to her father's surname before she marries (thus, Preissová was née Sekerová); afterwards, to her husband's name (thus, after her second marriage she was Halbaertová). The German and English title wording of the various Universal-Edition scores of *Jenůfa* call her Gabriele Preiss, but the form Preissová is used in every reference book, and in the New York Public Library catalogue.

[4]Occasionally a word repetition can be highly effective, when the music for the repetition is dramatically different. An outstanding example occurs at Laca's line "kterak ji lúbím" ("how I love her"; page 28); he first sings the words loud, roughly and sarcastically, but the repeat is quiet and to a gentle melody, revealing that the words are all too true.

[5]Apparently Czechs can readily understand Slovakian or Slovakian-tinged folksongs, just as almost any English-speaking child can cope with such Lowlands Scots as "for bonny Annie Laurie I'd lay me doon and dee."

[6]Hrazdira was also a composer. During his tenure as conductor in Brno from 1903 to 1907, he championed new works.

[7]Brod has been considered a relatively free translator, and his adaptation of *Vixen* is notorious for running counter to Janáček's intentions in major ways; but his rendering of *Jenůfa* is just about as faithful as the constraints of a singing translation allow, though it often calls for extra notes or rests in smaller type—the smaller type being used for the original Czech text!

[8]Still in 1924, Kleiber and Jurjewskaja made a truly memorable recording of Jenůfa's big solo scene in Act Two. The fastidious historian of bel canto, Michael Scott, considers it to be the soprano's best recording, adding (as recently as 1979!) that she amazingly performs sensitively and accurately music which is so "ugly" and badly written for the voice that it is no wonder if most singers just scream it with no steady pitch.

[9]From a different viewpoint, his career falls into three main phases—ethnographical, revolutionary, and autobiographical—with *Jenůfa* as the culmination of the first.

[10]Jealousy fascinated the composer, who as early as 1888 had written a male chorus called "Žárlivec" (The Jealous Man), in which a dying brigand attempts to kill his sweetheart so that she can never belong to another man.

[11]These recordings are said to represent the Prague tradition of performing *Jenůfa*, whereas the Brno tradition was truer to Janáček's original intentions. (Nevertheless, after the great Prague success of 1916, even Brno used Kovařovic, at least for a time.)

[12]Tyrrell, the executive editor of the 2001 edition of *Grove*, was born in 1942; his 1969 Oxford doctoral thesis was on Janáček, on whom he has written extensively.

Synopsis of the Opera

The main text of this synopsis, based on the original Czech, reflects only what is in the libretto and the vocal score (it is keyed to page numbers and cues, or rehearsal numbers, in the score). All additional comments and clarifications (chiefly derived from Preissová's uncut play) are in the notes at the end. (The earlier section on the characters should be read first.)

Act One

Late afternoon, outside the isolated Buryja mill, in mountainous terrain. Jenůfa is at the brook in the background. Her grandmother, in front of the shed, right, is peeling potatoes. Laca is sitting on a log, left, carving a whip handle.

Scene 1.[1] The curtain rises at cue ☐, p. 5. P. 6, ②: Jenůfa is scanning the horizon for Števa's return from the conscription board meeting in the village; she has been sleepless with worry, and prays to the Virgin: if Števa is taken and thus can't marry her, her shame will kill her. Her grandmother accuses her of shirking her work; her own old eyes are too weak. Laca says bitterly that her eyes are bad in many ways: she sees him merely as a hired hand, not as a relative; even when he was small, already orphaned, and craved affection, she neglected him and caressed her biological grandson, the golden-haired Števa. If she were now to give Laca the 1200 crowns coming to him,[2] he would leave for good. His grandmother resents his attitude, while Jenůfa upbraids him for his disrespect: how can he expect others to love him?

P. 13, ⑫: Laca asks his grandmother how she can put Jenůfa to work while she's so nervous about Števa.[3] Jenůfa remarks to herself on his keen insight into people's thoughts; but he's malicious and she won't respond to his words. She promises her grandmother to catch up with her work; she was just watering her pot of rosemary, which is withering; proverbially its drying up would mean an end to her happiness. The shepherd boy Jano, proud that he can now read a little, asks Jenůfa for more reading material, which she promises him; she'll also teach him to write, so he'll be a better man. Her grandmother praises her knowledge and her "man's brains," like her foster mother's (Jenůfa has also taught the servant girl Barena to read); in a long, significant musical passage, Jenůfa says that her intelligence has been swept away in the stream.

Scene 2. P. 23, ㉒: The mill foreman enters and admires Laca's carving; at Laca's request he takes the blunt knife and starts to sharpen it. With the unfinished whip handle Laca mischievously yanks Jenůfa's kerchief off her head; when she complains, he says she wouldn't mind if it were Števa doing it; she tells him to mind his own business. While she is briefly offstage, Laca converses with the foreman, who comments on Jenůfa's bewitching beauty, which Laca has obviously noticed himself! Laca says he loves her so much [the music contradicts his intended sarcasm] that he has put worms in her rosemary pot to make the plant wither, just as he wishes her marriage to Števa to be averted. The foreman says that Laca isn't that mean by nature; Jenůfa seems to bring out the worst in him.[4]

P. 31, ㉘: Laca gloats that Števa will never get Jenůfa if he's conscripted. But he hasn't been, declares the foreman, who has heard this news from the village. Jenůfa and her grandmother are overjoyed, Laca complains bitterly of the injustice of it all,[5] and the foreman envies Števa's constant good luck.[6] Amid this excitement, Jenůfa's stepmother, the sextoness, makes her first (very brief) entrance in the opera, commenting "So Števa wasn't conscripted" before entering the mill.[7] The foreman announces that the knife just won't get sharp, despite his efforts.

Scene 3. P. 36, ㉚: Jenůfa is reluctant to follow her mother into the mill. From offstage are heard the voices of the new recruits, beginning their song.[8]

Scene 4. P. 38, ㉛: The recruits' song states that most men wish to marry, and are afraid of war, whereas *they* feel just the opposite; rich men buy their way out of conscription, but poor men have to go. Števa's voice can now be heard joining in: "And that's an end to lovemaking!" The mill workers and maids come out, as Števa, the recruits, village musicians, and village boys (one with a toy trumpet) make a spectacular entrance.[9] Števa is blonde and handsome—also drunk—and his hat is decked with flowers.

Scene 5. P. 46, ⟨35⟩: Jenůfa gently reproaches Števa for being drunk yet again; he finds this reproach unbecoming to her: he's a rich landowner, and all the girls are crazy about him; he received his nosegay from one of them. Tossing coins to the musicians, he orders them to play Jenůfa's favorite song, "Far and Wide."[10] The chorus sings and dances this song, which is about a tower composed entirely of young lads; the sweetheart of the girl meant to be singing the song is placed atop the tower as its dome; when the dome-boy topples, the girl catches him in her lap. Next, Števa makes Jenůfa dance with him to the wild rhythm of an *odzemek*, until her stepmother interrupts the dance with an imperious wave of her hand.

P. 58, ⟨43⟩: That's how they'd be all their life if they married (she says), reckless paupers! That's the Buryja family style![11] Now she forbids the marriage for at least a year, during which Števa must prove he can stay sober; if Jenůfa doesn't obey, God will punish her. The recruits and the grandmother call the sextoness a hard woman.[12] Jenůfa is ordered to return home to the village the next day. Laca, delighted, kisses the sextoness' hand. She leaves, and the grandmother dismisses the musicians and the recruits, who have led her poor young Števa astray.

P. 66, ⟨55⟩: The grandmother consoles Jenůfa, saying: "Every couple must undergo its own suffering." (This one sentence is then repeated, in whole or in part, in an ensemble for soloists and chorus lasting six pages of the vocal score!)[13] Then everyone exits except Jenůfa and Števa.

Scene 6. P. 72, ⟨58⟩:[14] Jenůfa urges Števa not to antagonize her stepmother; she is afraid of having anyone discover her pregnancy before he marries her. The sextoness is so proud of her! Števa tells her to stop whining; he is angry at the sextoness' reprimands. When he reminds Jenůfa of how all the girls pursue him, she says that she alone has a right to him now; shaking him by the shoulders, she calls him weak and ridiculous. Trying to calm her, he calls her the prettiest of all; he loves her for her rosy "apple" cheeks. Their grandmother appears and tells him to go to bed; he exits with her.

Scene 7. P. 82, ⟨72⟩: Laca now enters, still holding his knife, and teases Jenůfa about how crestfallen the boastful Števa became when the sextoness lashed into him. Stung, Jenůfa replies that, nevertheless: Števa is a hundred times better than Laca. He picks up the nosegay that Števa dropped (a gift from another girl), and offers to attach it to Jenůfa's bodice. (The servant girl Barena now appears on the threshold.) Defiantly, Jenůfa says she'd be proud to wear something that was meant to honor Števa. Laca says that Števa sees nothing in her but her rosy cheeks, which a knife could spoil. When he tries to steal a kiss in return for the nosegay, Jenůfa resists; in the tussle he slashes her cheek and she runs off. Laca is dismayed: he has loved her since his boyhood. The grandmother and the foreman come running out; Barena assures them it was an accident; the foreman, sending the grandmother in to look after Jenůfa and to summon the sextoness, tells Laca, who is running away, that he's sure he did it on purpose.[15] The curtain falls quickly.

ACT TWO

Six months later. The main room in the sextoness' cottage. Many pictures and figurines of saints. A picture of the Virgin near the window. The curtain rises immediately before Scene 1.

Scene 1. P. 97: Jenůfa, her scar visible, is sewing by the table. Her stepmother, opening the bedroom door, asks why Jenůfa is constantly praying beside the window. Jenůfa says she can't help it, her mind is so restless. Ever since she was brought home, her stepmother says, she's been unhappy; the admission of her sin (to her stepmother only) saddened the older woman, too. Jenůfa has been kept in concealment,[16] and Števa has never come to ask about her. Her baby, named Števa (Števuška as a "diminutive" form of endearment) after his father, is now a week old, and Jenůfa loves him tenderly, whereas the sextoness wishes him out of the world (the child is a living symbol of her own disgrace, and she hates him for his resemblance to his despicable father). Jenůfa feels weak, and the sextoness gives her a potion to make her sleep better.[17] Jenůfa exits into the bedroom.

Scene 2. P. 111, ⟨17⟩: Left alone, the sextoness says that Števa hasn't come these twenty weeks, but she has sent for him today. All her praying and fasting for a miscarriage, a stillbirth, or the infant's death has been in vain; now she must give Jenůfa to Števa, who will make her miserable, and she, the sextoness, must humble herself in front of him. She locks the bedroom door when she hears someone outside.[18]

xv

Scene 3. P. 115, [21]: Števa enters and asks why he was sent for. The sextoness informs him that his son has been born. Števa says he had often thought about Jenůfa, and felt bad about her, but was prevented from coming by the recollection of the sextoness' reprimand and the spoiling of Jenůfa's beauty. The sextoness, revealing that Jenůfa was never in Vienna, as she had given out, asks Števa to enter the bedroom and look at mother and child.[19] He doesn't, but he offers to pay all costs, as long as no one is told that the child is his. The sextoness kneels before him, begging him to look at his son and to rescue the honor of both women. Števa says he's afraid of Jenůfa, who has now become as stern and gloomy as the sextoness; his love disappeared when her looks were ruined; he also fears the sextoness, whom he likens to a persecuting witch. He announces his engagement to the mayor's daughter. When Jenůfa cries out in her sleep that a stone has fallen on her, the sextoness' attention is diverted, and Števa escapes. The sextoness is at the height of fury against both father and son.

Scene 4. P. 132, [46]: Laca, who has frequently visited the sextoness for news of Jenůfa "in Vienna," now arrives; having caught sight of Števa departing, he realizes Jenůfa must be home. Learning that Števa has rejected her, he asks for her hand (the sextoness has always been good to him). To test his love, the sextoness tells him about the baby. When he balks momentarily at accepting Števa's baby along with Jenůfa, she impulsively says that it has died, and that Števa is aware of the fact. She feverishly sends Laca away, on the pretext that she must know when Števa's wedding is to take place.[20] He promises to return in a moment.

Scene 5 (the sextoness' great monologue). P. 139, [56]: That brief moment, the sextoness says, will be an eternity for her. If she tries to hide the baby, people will find out and her good name will be besmirched. Wrapping a shawl around herself, she announces that she will take the baby to God; if she puts it under the ice in the river, there will be no trace left by spring thaw. Becoming delirious, she imagines people finding out and attacking her and Jenůfa: "See her, the sextoness?" She dashes into the bedroom and returns with the well-wrapped baby.

Scene 6 (Jenůfa's great monologue). P. 146, [61]: As her stepmother rushes out, locking the front door, Jenůfa enters; she is groggy from the potion, and her thoughts are disjointed. It takes her a while to recall her concealment and her whereabouts. Since it's now dark, it's all right for her to open the window; she admires the moon, which "shines for the unfortunate." She still hopes for Števa to come. Now she notices that the baby is missing, and thinks he's been kidnapped and is suffering from the cold. Then she believes that her stepmother has taken him to the mill to show him off, and she becomes a little calmer. She prays to the Virgin (most of the text is a Czech adaptation of the "Salve regina"),[21] asking to protect little Števuška.

Scene 7. P. 157, [78]: The sextoness returns; too distraught to open the front door herself, she passes the key to Jenůfa through the window. When Jenůfa asks about the baby, she says that Jenůfa has been in a fever for two days, during which time her son died. Jenůfa is crushed, though the child may be better off dead. Her stepmother says she should thank God for making her free again; Jenůfa is to forget about Števa, and curse him; the sextoness reports how she knelt before him, while he offered only money and insulted the two women. Jenůfa asks God to forgive him. The sextoness tells her of Števa's engagement, and urges her to look favorably on Laca, who knows about the baby and forgives her.

Scene 8. P. 166, [90]: Laca returns, saying that no one was home at the mayor's house. Jenůfa thanks Laca for his concern; she heard him from her bedroom every time he came to call; she had imagined a different life for herself, but at least she is now at the end of it. The sextoness assures Laca that Jenůfa will accept him, but Jenůfa stresses her shame and the fact that she can't love Laca with the same ardor that she had felt for Števa. Laca still wants her. The sextoness feels that her own actions have been for the best; she gives the couple her blessing, which, in her agitation, degenerates into a wild curse on Števa and his coming marriage: "Woe to him and to me!" A gust of wind blows the window open, and she thinks she hears a cry. At her request, Jenůfa shuts the window. The sextoness says: "It was as if death had peered in!" The curtain falls quickly.[22]

Scene 1. P. 178: Same set as in Act Two; it is two months later. Simple decorations for a quiet wedding celebration. Jenůfa in a bridal dress. Laca, his grandmother, the shepherdess (her first appearance in the opera), and the very agitated sextoness are also present.

The curtain rises at ④, p. 181. The shepherdess asks Jenůfa if she isn't apprehensive about marrying (the answer is no), because brides traditionally hate to lose their freedom, but she then remembers that her own husband proved to be a good, kind man.

Scene 2. P. 184, ⑥: The mayor and his wife arrive (their first appearance in the opera), and are struck by the poor state of the usually self-assured sextoness' mental and physical health; they say that their daughter Karolka will soon arrive with Števa, her fiancé. The sextoness says she's glad of Jenůfa's wedding, but she herself is pining away and can't sleep. When Jenůfa assures her she'll get well again, she replies that she doesn't want to; long life would be a horror, "and, after that, what?" The mayor's wife asks why Jenůfa is dressed so demurely, and the sextoness says that the finest ladies get married in simple attire.[23] The mayor's wife is unconvinced. The sextoness invites her and her husband to inspect the trousseau in the bedroom. Only Jenůfa and Laca remain.

Scene 3. P. 192, ⑮: Laca has brought a bouquet for Jenůfa, who says he deserves a better bride; he insists he loves her without qualification, that he had immediately gotten over his first shock at her transgression. He promises to spend his life atoning for disfiguring her; she thanks him for standing by her when Števa had deserted her. Laca, who had hated Števa, has forgiven him at Jenůfa's pleading, and has invited him to the wedding.

Scene 4. P. 198, ㉔: Števa and Karolka arrive; Karolka is superficial and chirpy: she says that they are late because Števa dragged his feet so. Her own wedding is imminent. She thinks it's a shame that there's no music at Jenůfa's. Jenůfa asks the stepbrothers to shake hands; each of them has a good quality, she says: Števa is handsome and Laca has a kind soul. Karolka urges her not to praise Števa; he's conceited enough already! "He's still so childish?" Jenůfa asks. Števa's wedding is only two weeks off. Karolka says jokingly that she may still turn him down; people are warning her about him; Števa says he'd kill himself if she did. Jenůfa says he has now found the right woman for him, and wishes that his new love may never do him harm.

Scene 5. P. 203, ㉜: The others come back in, the mayor quietly complaining about the overlong trousseau viewing, and the sextoness dismayed at Števa's unlucky presence.

Scene 6. P. 205, ㉝: Barena arrives with village girls who wish to sing a bridesmaids' song, even though they haven't been invited; they promise not to stay long. They sing the song "Ej, mamko" (Oh, Mother) [unlike the two songs in Act One, this one was in the original play], a dialogue between a girl and her mother: the girl wants a new dress to be married in; her mother replies that she's too young; the girl retorts that her mother was eager to marry at the same age. The mayor praises their song. Laca says that he and Jenůfa are expected in church. The couple kneel to receive their grandmother's blessing. Next, it's the sextoness' turn to bless them, but she's interrupted by voices outside: a child has been murdered by some monster.

Scene 7. P. 216, ㊴: Jano enters and reports that men cutting ice for the brewery found a frozen baby, its body, clothing, and wrappings well preserved; people are gathering to lament.

Scene 8. P. 219, ㊶: All run out, except the sextoness, the grandmother, and Števa, even though the sextoness urges Jenůfa to stay. The sextoness is afraid of people coming after her; the grandmother thinks her mind is wandering. Števa tries to run away, but Karolka meets him at the door and seizes his arm.

Scene 9. P. 222, ㊸: Karolka says that if this were her own wedding day, she'd weep. From outside Jenůfa is heard: she recognizes the baby as her own. Laca leads her in, begging her not to say such weird, horrible things. The mayor enters, carrying the baby's clothes. The others follow him. The front door remains open, and villagers look in.

Scene 10. P. 224, ④⑤: Jenůfa wonders how anyone had had the heart to leave the baby without a coffin or a wreath. The onlookers begin to accuse her of the murder, and want to stone her. The mayor reluctantly feels he must arrest her. Laca protects her, vowing to kill anyone who comes near her. Now the sextoness rises with difficulty, stating that she alone knows the truth: she did it to save Jenůfa's life and happiness, ashamed that her careful upbringing of her foster daughter had led only to disgrace; she couldn't bear the loss of two lives because of the child, and she had hidden Jenůfa at home, then drugged her and carried the baby to the river, shoving it through a hole in the ice; afterwards she had lied to Jenůfa about its death. Hearing about the ice, Jenůfa is disgusted and furious, and orders her stepmother to leave her alone. Karolka realizes it has all been Števa's fault, and she leaves him; her mother takes her home; the shepherdess says that no girl will have him now, not even a self-respecting Gypsy.[24] Laca blames himself for it all: if he hadn't disfigured Jenůfa, Števa would have married her. Števa leaves, and the shepherdess leads the grandmother out.

Scene 11. P. 238, ⑤⑤: Jenůfa now forgives her stepmother, for whom humiliation and torments are in store.[25] The sextoness starts to dash into the bedroom [presumably to kill herself], but changes her mind: she must clear Jenůfa of the murder at the trial. Jenůfa realizes that her stepmother had acted out of love for her. Laca thinks she's crazy to forgive her, but Jenůfa says that the Savior will look down upon her stepmother mercifully. The sextoness asks only for Jenůfa's forgiveness; she now knows that she loved herself more than she loved Jenůfa,[26] who will no longer call her "mother dear"; Jenůfa, who was unable to inherit the sextoness' courage, is now lending her her strength. The mayor leads the sextoness away. Eleven C-major chords are followed by a long fermata.

Scene 12 [like an epilogue/apotheosis].[27] P. 244. Jenůfa and Laca are alone. She asks him to go, because she is now too far below him; he is the finest man she ever met. She forgave the disfigurement long ago, since he had sinned for love, just as she had with Števa. Laca asks if she is really going out into the world in search of a better life without taking him along. She says she will have to appear at the trial, where her name will be dragged through the mud. Laca says he can endure that for her sake, as long as they're together. Now Jenůfa loves him unreservedly. She says: "Now I have been led to you by that higher love which satisfies God."[28] Their love music continues for another eleven measures after the fall of the curtain.

S. A.

---

[1]Each act in *Jenůfa* is a continuous action in one locale. A scene change refers not to a change of locale, a curtain, or a blackout, but to the significant entrance or exit of one or more characters.

[2]The play explains that this was his late father's share in the mill. The money is never mentioned again, even in the play.

[3]In the play, he adds that Jenůfa would have already run to the village to meet Števa were it not that her stepmother was expected at the mill to fetch butter. This is the first mention of the sextoness in the play; her later entrance is thus explained much better than in the libretto.

[4]In the play, the conversation between Laca and the foreman is much longer, and rather clumsily provides a lot of background information for the audience (which the characters themselves must already know). Among other things, the foreman says that Števa is a spendthrift, like Jenůfa's father, and is incapable of running the mill as well as Laca could.

[5](In the play): Though Laca is weaker physically than Števa, he has put in his three years in the army. It is also mentioned that Števa has already jilted two other girls.

[6]Janáček's audience must have been familiar with current conscription proceedings. Without such knowledge, it is hard to say whether Števa's good luck consisted in not having been chosen by lot, or in his ability to buy himself off.

[7]In the play, she had already appeared and had shared a long expository scene with the mayor's wife; in the course of that scene, the sextoness says she is preparing a very fine trousseau for Jenůfa, whom she has raised perfectly.

[8]This conscripts' song, newly set to an old text, does not appear in the original play.

[9]In the play, the mill staff do not appear (Janáček wanted them for a big mixed chorus); on the other hand, the mayor and his wife are in the group that enters; she upbraids him for his drunkenness and profligacy, and the two of them soon depart.

[10]Not performed in the play, where another song is named as Jenůfa's favorite, but not sung. The words of "Far and Wide," however, do occur (in a different situation) in the short novel that Preissová later derived from her play.

[11]Just before ⑮, Universal-Edition scores since 1969 have restored, as an option, a long cut (eight pages of vocal score) in the sextoness' speech (beginning "Aji on byl zlatohřivý" [Ah, he was golden-maned]) that Janáček himself made voluntarily before the very first vocal score of 1908 (it is unclear how often, if at all, it had been performed before that). The sextoness explains her objections to the marriage: Her own husband, Števa's uncle, was blonde and handsome, and she longed for him even before his first marriage (to Jenůfa's mother); when he became widowed, she married him, though her mother warned her not to. He drank, ran into debt, beat her, and frequently drove her out of the house. Števa is like him, and not good enough for Jenůfa; she, the sextoness, hadn't objected earlier because Jenůfa was so obviously in love with him. (Since the 1970s this cut has frequently been restored in performance.)

[12]And, in the play, the grandmother, who always pampers Števa, defends the memory of his uncle as well.

[13]When a critic complained about this orgy of word repetition, Janáček's defense was not particularly cogent.

[14]This scene is strikingly reminiscent of the confrontation between Santuzza and Turiddu in Mascagni's *Cavalleria rusticana* (1890). Preissová couldn't have known the opera when she wrote her play, but *Cavallerìa* had already existed as a story and a famous play (both by Giovanni Verga). Janáček definitely knew the opera when he wrote *Jenůfa*, since he had reviewed a performance of it in Brno in 1892.

[15]In the play, the foreman also promises Laca not to testify against him, nevertheless. Here, Janáček's cut in the text makes for a more effective close to the act.

[16]The play adds at this point that the sextoness had given out the false information that Jenůfa was working as a servant in Vienna. When her alleged stay in Vienna is mentioned later in the libretto, it is never stated what she was supposed to be doing there.

[17]The play specifies that it has been brewed from poppies.

[18]Here Janáček omitted a long scene between the sextoness and the shepherdess, who has come to get a remedy for an ailment. The sextoness shows her Jenůfa's trousseau. The shepherdess reports that Števa has become engaged to Karolka, the mayor's daughter; the sextoness assures her that Jenůfa still has Laca to fall back on.

[19]In the play, she blames herself for having sent Jenůfa to work at the mill, with all those men around, under the inadequate supervision of her doddering grandmother.

[20]In the play, she sends him specifically to the mayor's house.

[21]The moment is reminiscent of Desdemona's "Ave Maria" in Verdi's *Otello* (1887). In her 1959 volume of reminiscences, a former maid of Janáček's, either lying or else suffering from an acute lapse of memory, claimed that the composer wanted to add the hymn to his libretto, and that she supplied him with the words from her prayerbook when he couldn't remember them. But the entire hymn is in Preissová's play! Other statements by this maid have tacitly entered the general literature on *Jenůfa*, but are deserving of the deepest suspicion.

[22]Here (again) Janáček wisely cut some additional dialogue, allowing the orchestra to repeat obsessively the rhythm of the sextoness' final word in the act (set to five identical notes).

[23]The copyright-1993 Universal full score here restores a tiny textual cut made by Kovařovic: "What's good enough for them is good enough for Jenůfa."

[24]The stigma attached to a villager's liaison with a Gypsy is made abundantly clear in Janáček's song cycle *Zápisník zmizelého* (The Missing Man's Notebook; usually rendered as "Diary of One Who Disappeared"; composed 1917–1919).

[25]She will surely be sentenced to death.

[26](The play adds): Because she had put her own pride first; a true mother would have shared her daughter's shame more readily.

[27]The ethereal beauty of this last scene, ushered in by harps, is reminiscent of the placid, otherworldly music in the final (tomb) scene in Verdi's *Aïda* (1871).

[28]Here again, Janáček's sure instincts led him to eliminate further dialogue contained in the play.

CONTENTS

JENŮFA

Vocal Score

INSTRUMENTS INDICATED IN THE VOCAL SCORE

When the vocal score mentions orchestral instruments and voice ranges, the terms are sometimes in Italian, sometimes in German, with no obvious rationale for the choice. The following is an alphabetical list of these terms, exactly as they appear in the vocal score:

Alt: [chorus] altos

Arpa: harp(s)

Bariton: baritone [offstage voice]

Bass: [chorus] basses

Bassi: string basses

Bkl: bass clarinet

con sord.: muted

Cor.: horns

Ehr.: English horn

Fag.: bassoons

Fl.: flute(s)

Kl., Klar.: clarinet(s)

Ob.: oboe(s)

Picc.: piccolo

Sop., Sopran: [chorus and offstage] soprano(s)

Ten., Tenor: [chorus] tenors

Timp.: timpani

Trbe.: trumpets

Trbni.: trombones

Viol., Vl.: violin(s)

Vla: violas

Vlc.: cellos

Xylophon: xylophone

All tempi, dynamics, etc., are in standard musical Italian.

JENUFA.

JEJÍ PASTORKYŇA.
(Ihre Ziehtochter.)

1. Akt.

Spätnachmittag. Einsame Mühle im Gebirge. Rechts vor dem Haus ein Vorbau aus Holzpfählen. Berghang, Gebüsch, ein paar gefällte Baumstämme, hinten die Bachrinne.

Jenufa, einen Topf mit Rosmarin im Arm, steht beim Bach. Sie späht unter ihrer Handfläche in die Ferne hinaus.

Die alte Buryja sitzt vor dem Vorbau, nimmt Kartoffel aus einem vollgehäuften Korb, schneidet die Augen heraus und wirft die Kartoffel in einen zweiten Korb.

Links sitzt auf einem Baumstrunk der dunkelhaarige Laca; schält und schnitzt mit seinem Messer einen Peitschenstiel zurecht.

Jednání I.

Podvečer. Osamělý, pohorský mlýn. V pravo před domovním stavením siňka z dřevěných sloupů. Stráňka, křoviny, několik pokácených dřev, v zadu strouha.

Jenůfa, květináč rozmarije v ruce, stojí na vyvýšeném místě u struhy a z pod dlaně pohlíží do dálky.

Stařenka sedí v siňce vybírajíc brambory z vrchovatého koše, vykrajuje očka a hází do nůše.

V levo na pokáceném stromě sedí tmavovlasý Laca; ořezává křivákem bičíště.

1. Szene.
Die Alte, Laca, Jenufa, später der Schäferjunge **Jano.**

Výstup I.
Stařenka, Laca, Jenůfa, (později) pasák **Jano.**

2 Jenufa (für sich).
Jenůfa (k sobě).

Ach, es wird schon A-bend und Ste-wa ist nicht zu-rück,
Už se ve-čer chý-lí a Šte-vo se ne-vra-cí

ppp dolcissimo
con Ped. sempre
una corda

und Ste-wa ist nicht zu-rück! Wie mich die Angst ge-
a Šte-vo se ne-vra-cí! Hrů-za se va mně

stringendo cresc.
pp
cresc.

schüt-telt hat, heut' in der Nacht, und mor-gens fing's wie-der an mich zu
vě-ša-la po ce-lou noc, a co jsem se rá-na do-cka-la,

cresc.

a tempo
(verzweifelt)
(zoufale)

quä-len!... Jung-frau Ma-ri-a,
z no va!... O Pan-no Ma-ri-a,

p
fp   a tempo
Ob.
tre corde
Klar.

wenn du's nicht ab-wen-den willst, wenn sie den Liebsten mir zu den Sol-da-ten tun
jest-lis mne os-ly-se-la, jest-li mi fra-je-ra na voj-nu se-bra-li

Vl.
fp

7

8

10

12

14

Will dem Kerl lie-ber kei-ne Ant - wort ge - ben__
A - ni mu od - po - ri-dat ne - bu-du zlo-cho - vi.__

(zur Alten)
(K stařence)

Müt - ter - chen,   ärgert Euch nur nicht,
Sta - řen - ko,   ne-hně-vej - te se

Müt-ter-chen, är - gert Euch nur nicht!   Ger - ne will ich
sta-řen-ko, ne - hně - vej - te se!   Já to vše - cko

dop - pelt schaf - fen,   ger - ne, ger - ne dop - pelt schaf - fen.
vy - na - hra - dím,   vše - cko, vše - cko vy - na - hra - dím

15

16

18

22

2. Szene.
Der Altgesell und die Vorigen.

Výstup II.
Stárek a předešli.

22 **Allegro.** (♩ = 76.)

Altgesell (in städtischen mehlbestaubten Kleidern_ geht vorbei, bleibt vor **Laca** stehen).
Stárek (v městských, moukou pobílených šatech kráčí kolem a zastaví se u Lacy).

Was für Ar-beit, La - ca?
Co to ro - bíš, mlád - ku?

Laca.
Stumpf ist das
Mám tu-pý

Wird wohl ein Peit-schenstiel dar-aus!
Mů - že být pěk - né bi - čiš - tě!

Mes - ser,
kři - vák,
nie-mals krieg'ich so die Ar-beit fer - tig!
a - bych se s tím dvě ho - di - ny pá - ral!

Schleif' es mir!
Na - brus mi ho!

24

26

28

32

34

36

3. Szene.
Jenufa, die Alte u. Chor.
Výstup III.
Jenůfa, Stařenka a sbor.

38

4. Szene.
Jenufa, die alte Buryja, Laca, Stewa, Altgesell, (später) Küsterin u. Chor.

Výstup IV.
Jenůfa, Stařenka, Laca, Števa, Stárek, (později) Kostelnička a sbor.

40

42

43

46

48

49

50

(Der Tanz geht weiter.)
(v tanci se pokračuje)

52

St.
Št.

auf den Turm drauf-pas-sen, mußt er den Turm-knauf gar aus sich ma-chen las - sen.
na sám vř - šek da - li, zla - tú ma - ko - věn-ku z ně-ho u - dě - la - li.

auf den Turm drauf-pas-sen, mußt er den Turm-knauf gar aus sich ma-chen las - sen.
na sám vř - šek da - li, zla - tú ma - ko - věn-ku z ně-ho u - dě - la - li.

auf den Turm drauf-pas-sen, mußt er den Turm-knauf gar aus sich ma-chen las - sen.
na sám vř - šek da - li, zla - tú ma - ko - věn-ku z ně-ho u - dě - la - li.

auf den Turm drauf-pas-sen, mußt er den Turm-knauf gar aus sich ma-chen las - sen.
na sám vř - šek da - li, zla - tú ma - ko - věn-ku z ně-ho u - dě - la - li.

(Der Tanz geht weiter.)
(v tanci se pokračuje)

54

(Der Tanz geht weiter.)
(v tanci se pokračuje)

58

60

62

64

68

69

6. Szene.

Jenufa, Stewa, später die Alte.

Výstup VI.

Jenůfa, Števa, později Stařenka.

Recit.
Jenufa (ruhig zu Stewa).
Jenůfa (tiše k Ştevovi).

Ste — wa, Ste-wa, ich weiß, — heu-te hast du das aus
Šte — vo, Šte-vo, já vím, žes to u-ro-bil

Allegro. (♩ = 144.)

Freu-de nur ge- tan. Doch er- zürn' die Mut- ter nicht,
z té ra-do-sti dnes. A-le jin-da, Šte-vuš-ko,

f espress.

Ste — wa, nicht noch ein-mal; kennst ja mein E-lend, kennst
ne-knč- vej ma-mi-čku; viš, jak jsem běd-ná, viš,

rit.   a tempo

ja mein E-lend! Ban-ge, ja bang schlägt das
jak jsem běd-ná! Sr-dce mi úz- ko-stú

74

78

7. Szene.
Laca, Jenufa; (später,) **Barena, Altgesell, die Alte.**
Výstup VII.
Laca, Jenůfa; (později,) **Barena, Stárek, Stařenka.**

84

Schau' mal,
O - kaž_

willst dir ihn wohl in das Mie - der stek - ken...
já ti ji za - str - čím za kor - dul - ku...

(Barena, die Dienstmagd, zeigt sich auf der Schwelle.)
(Děvečka Barena vyjde na práh.)

Cor.

Jenufa (erhebt sich trotzig).
Jenůfa (povstane hrdě).

Gib ihn her!
Dej ji sem!

G.-P.

86

88

90

93

2. Akt.

Slowakische Bauernstube. Die Wände mit Heiligenbildern und Statuetten bedeckt; bei der Türe ein kleiner Weihkessel. Ofen, Bett mit hoch aufgeschichteten Federbetten, Truhe, Geschirrschrank, einige Sessel. Beim Fenster ein Muttergottesbild.

Jednání II.

Slovenská jizba. Stěny pokryty obrázky a soškam;i u dveří kropenka. Kamna, ustlaná postel, truhla, bidélko na šaty. Polička s nádobím, několik židlic. U okna zavěšen obraz Bohorodičky.

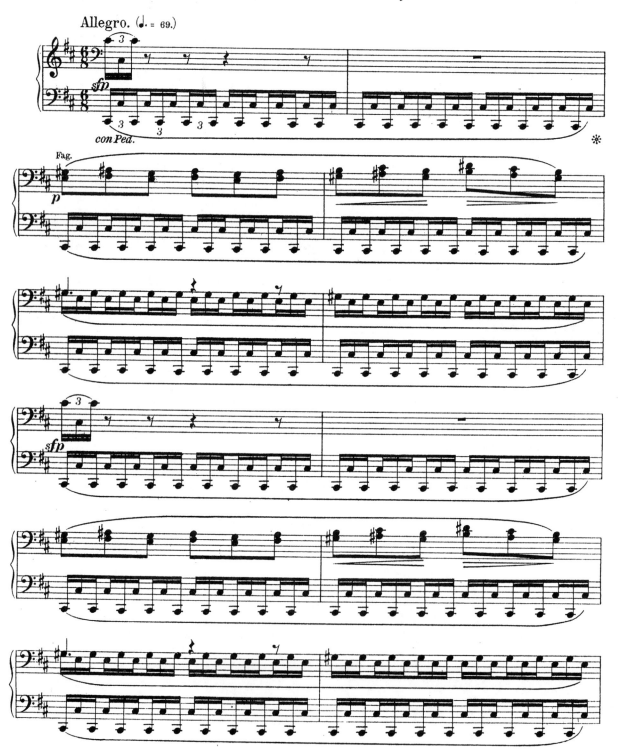

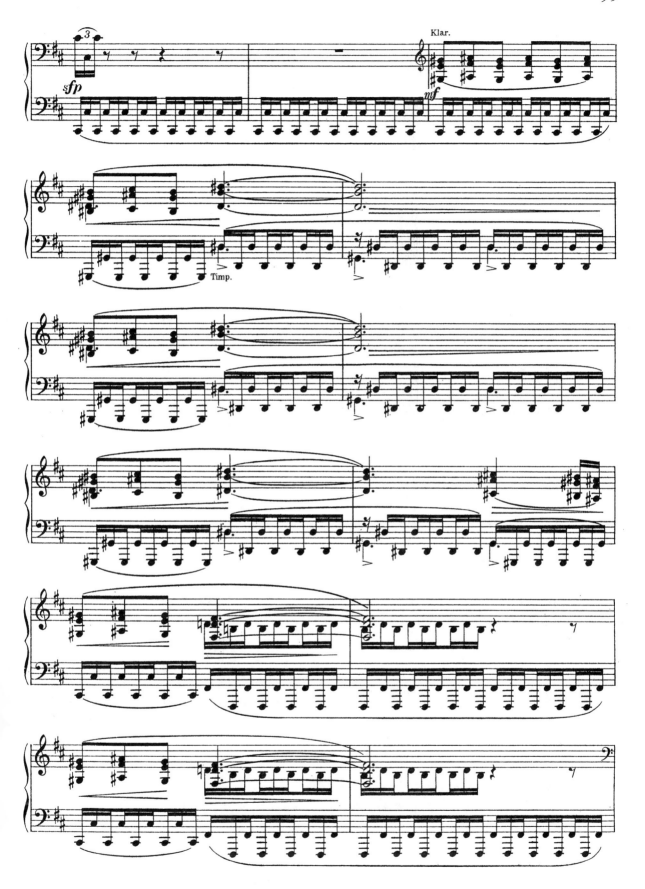

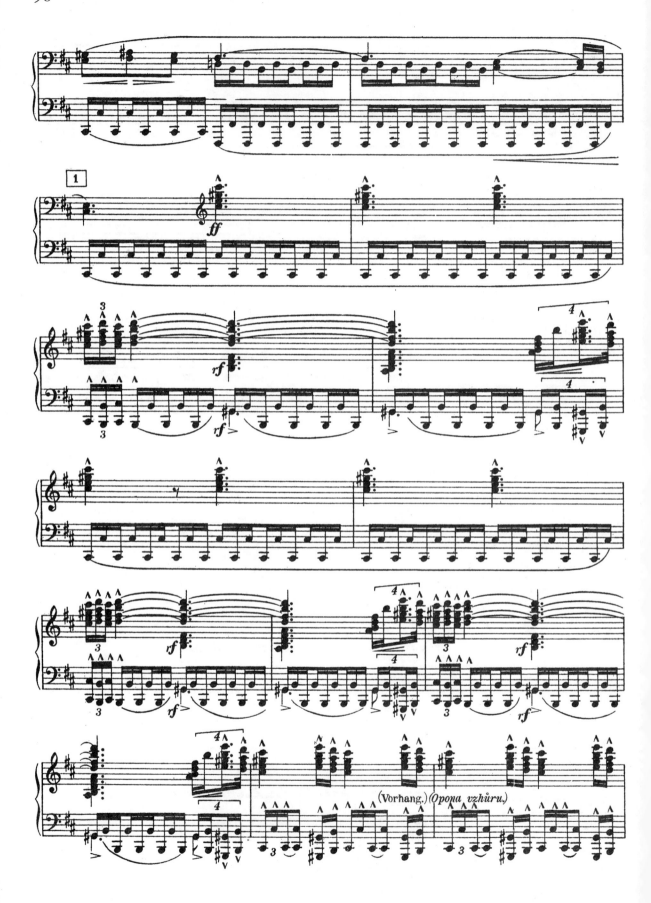

97

1. Szene.
Jenufa, die Küsterin.
Výstup I.
Jenůfa, Kostelnička.

(Jenufa im Hauskleid, bleich, die Schramme im Gesicht noch bemerkbar. Sie sitzt beim Tisch und näht, das Haupt gesenkt.)
(*Jenůfa v domácím obleku s pobledlou tváří, na níž je zřejmá jizva, sedí na židli u stolku a se sklonénou hlavou šije.*)

(Die Küsterin nähert sich der Seitentüre zur Kammer, öffnet sie.)
(*Kostelnička blíží se k postranním dveřím komory a otevře je.*)

Küsterin.
Kostelnička.

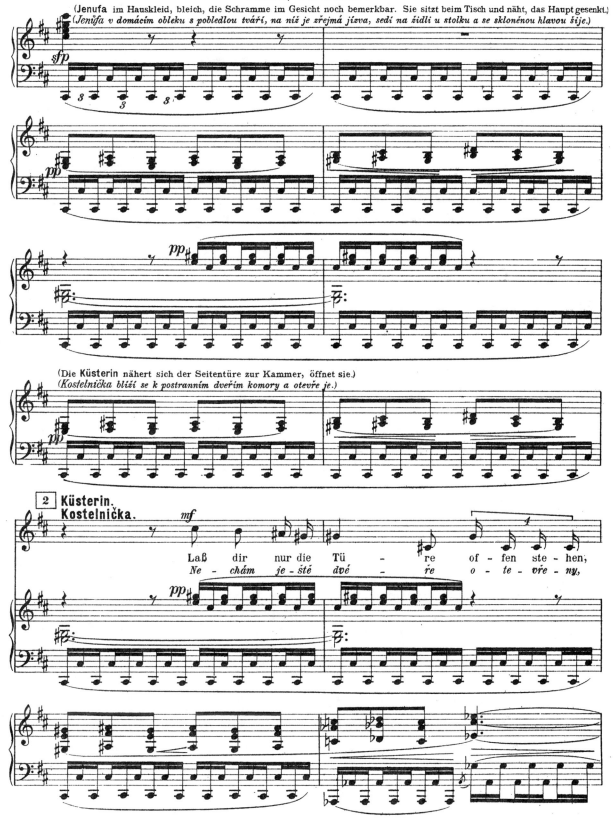

Laß dir nur die Tü - re of - fen ste - hen;
Ne - chám je -ště dve - ře o - te - vře - ny,

98

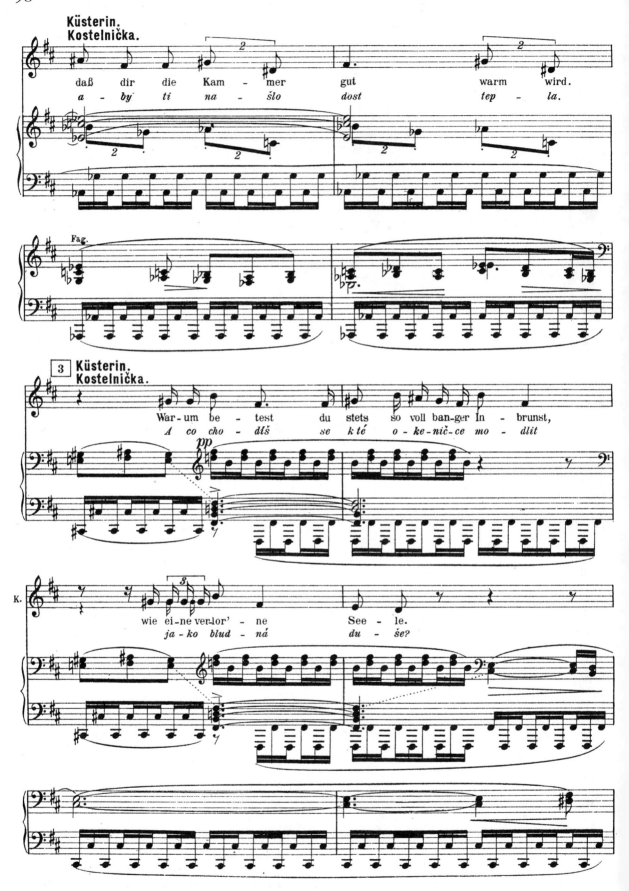

Küsterin.
Kostelnička.

daß dir die Kam - mer gut warm wird.
a - by ti na - šlo dost tep - la.

Fag.

3 **Küsterin.**
Kostelnička.

War - um be - test du stets so voll ban-ger In - brunst,
A co cho - díš se k té o - ke - nič - ce mo - dlit

pp

K.

wie ei-ne ver-lor' - ne See - le.
ja - ko blud - ná du - še?

100

8 Meno mosso. (♩ = 63.)

pp tremolando

dolce con espressione

Vla. Kl.

Küsterin.
Kostelnička.

Im - mer die-se Zärt-lich-kei - ten,
Po - řád se stím dé-ckem ma-žeš,

K.

soll-test auf den Knie_ en un-sern Herr-gott lie-ber bit - ten,
mí - sto a - bys Pá-na - bo-ha, Pá-na - bo-ha pro-si - la,

9

K.

daß er dir das Kind bald neh-me,
by ti u - leh-čil od né-ho!

daß er dir das Kind bald neh-me!
by ti u - leh-čil od né-ho!

Ob.

106

108

(Jenufa trinkt aus und geht langsam in die Kammer.)
(*Jenůfa vypije odchází.*)

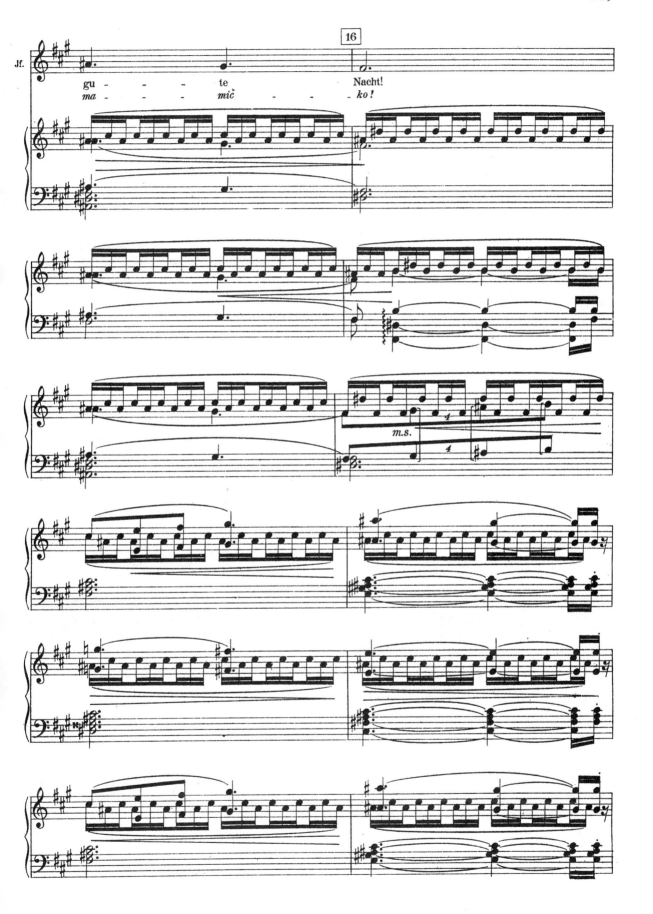

110

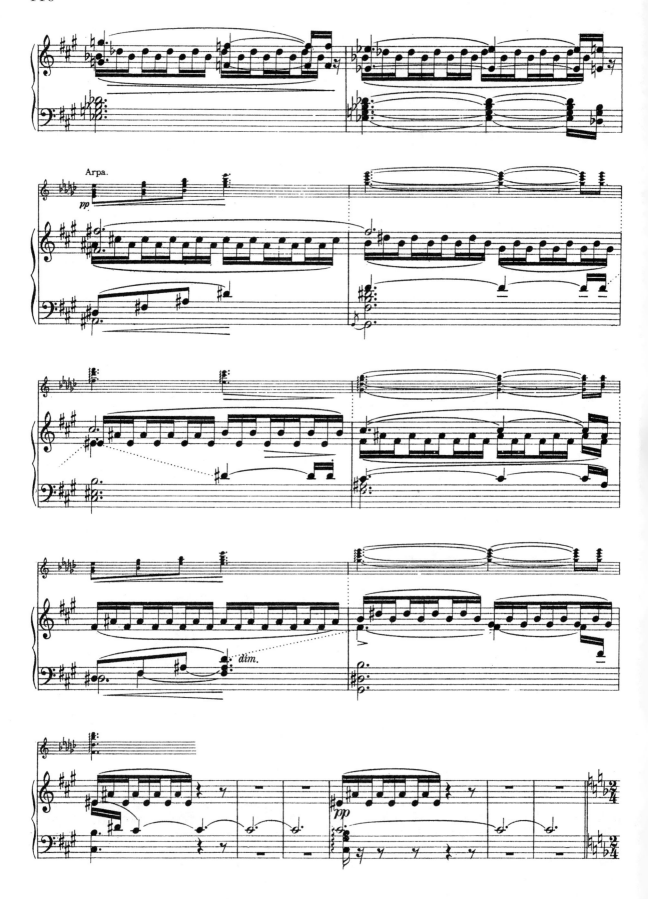

2. Szene.
Küsterin (allein.)

Výstup II.
Kostelnička (sama.)

112

114

#

3. Szene.
Stewa, Küsterin.

Výstup III.
Števa, Kostelnička.

116

118

und ver - dros - sen   hat's mich   recht.
a   mr - ze - lo   mne   to   dost.

Und wie Ihr mich   da - mals ge-schol-ten habt,
A když jste se   na   mne tak o - sáp - la,—

und wie Ihr mich   da - mals ge-schol-ten habt,
a když jste se   na   mne tak o - sáp - la,—

120

122

124

126

128

130

134

136

5. Szene.
Küsterin (allein.)

Výstup V.
Kostelnička (sama.)

142

144

146

147

148

150

152

158

160

162

166

8. Szene
Laca, die Vorigen.

Výstup VIII.
Laca. Předešlé.

169

172

173

174

178

3. Akt.

Die Stube der Küsterin wie im 2. Akt. Weißes Tischtuch auf dem Tische, ein Rosmarinstrauß, einige Rosmarinbüschel mit Bändern auf einem Teller. Eine Flasche Wein, Gläser, auf einem Teller Kuchen (Kolatschen).

1. Szene.

Küsterin, Jenufa, Laca, die Alte Buryja, eine Magd.

Jenufa sitzt am Tisch, sie ist festlich gekleidet, hat Gebetbuch und Taschentuch in der Hand. Die Magd bindet ihr das Kopftuch. Bei Jenufa steht Laca. Auf einem Sessel beim Tisch sitzt die Alte Buryja. Die Küsterin geht in fieberhafter Erregung auf und ab. Man merkt ihr die Seelenqual an. Jenufa sieht blühender aus als im 2. Akt, aber ernst.

Jednání III.

Jizba Kostelničina z druhého jednání. Na stole bílé prostěradlo a květináč s rozmaryjí, několik proutků opentlené rozmaryje na talíři. Láhev vina, několik sklínek a talíř koláčů.

Výstup I.

Kostelnička, Jenůfa, Laca, Stařenka, Pastuchyňa.

Jenůfa sedí na židli, svátečně ustrojená, modlitby a šátek v ruce. Pastuchyňa jí pozadu uvazuje šátek na hlavě. U Jenůfy stojí Laca. U stolu na židli sedí Stařenka ze mlýna. Kostelnička přechází jevic horečný nepokoj a vnitřní muka; jest velmi přepadlá a schvácená. Jenůfa vyhlíží svěžeji než v jednání II., ale vážně.

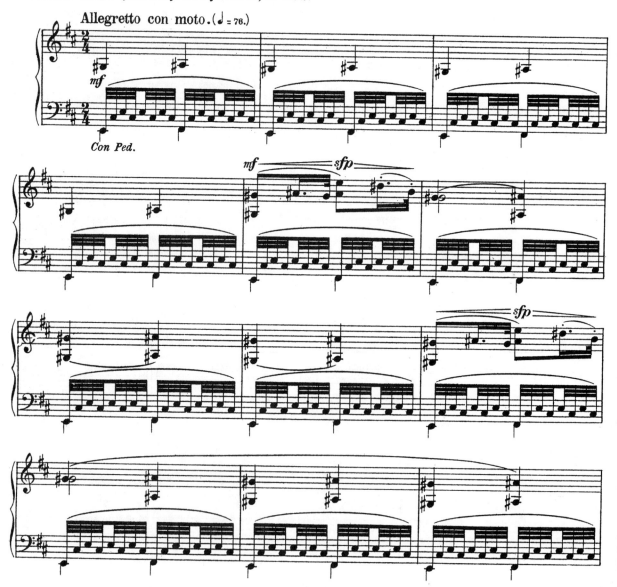

184

M.
P.

Gott grüß euch!
Ví - taj - te!

R.

Ka-rol-ka wird dann gleich mit ih - rem Ste - wa kom - men.
Ka-rol-ka jen co se do-čká Ště-vy, při-jdou spo-lu.

Jenufa (erhebt sich).
Jenůfa *(povstane).* f

Will-kom - men!
Ví - taj - te!

Laca. f

Hoch die Gä - ste!
Zdrá-vi do - šli!

pp

Magd (für sich, leicht).
Pastuchyňa *(lehce, u stolu).*

(Schenkt ein und verteilt die Rosmarinsträuß-
(Podává na zavdanou a potom rozmaryju.) chen.)

Seit ih-rer Krankheit ist die Kü-ste-rin im Kop-fe so schwach!
Ko-stel - ni - čka je po-řád po ne - mo - ci sla-bé-ho du - cha.

cresc.

Richter.
f **Rychtář.**

Frei - lich, das muß man se - hen, da geht's ab - wärts!
Vi - dét to po ni, hy - ne, hy - ne jak - si!

mf

186

187

188

190

Richterin.
Rychtářka.

Herrschaft her, Herrschaft hin, laßt sie mo-disch sein, wir auf dem Land sind and-re Men-schen,
Pá - ni si dě - la - jí vše - cko po mo - dách, a - le my ta - dy na dě - di - ně,

wir auf dem Land sind and-re Men-schen! Nein, ich wär' nie-mals oh-ne Band und Kranz zum
a - le my ta - dy na dě - di - ně! No, já bych ku ol - tá - ři by - la ne - šla

Trau-al-tar ge - gan-gen, ich wär' nie - mals so ge - gan-gen, nicht um die
bez věn-ce a pan-tli, ne - šla, ne - šla, ne - šla, ne - šla, a - ni za

Welt so in die Kir - che, nie-mals!
ti - síc rýns kých, ne - šla, ne - šla!

192

193

194

196

198

200

202

6. Szene.

Die Vorigen, Barena und die Dorfmädchen.

(Sie bringen einen Rosmarinbuschen und einen mit Bändern geschmückten Blumenstrauß.)

Výstup VI.

Předešlí, Barena s děvčaty.

(Přináší kytici z rozmaryje a květu muškátu, ověšenou barevnými stužkami.)

206

208

210

212

214

Die Alte.
Staŕenka.

Nehmt mei - nen Se - gen im
Tož já vám že - hnám,

Na - men des Va - ters und des Soh-nes und des heil-gen Gei-stes.
ve jmé-nu Ot - ce, Sy - na aj Du - cha sva - té - ho.

(Das Brautpaar küßt die
Hände der alten Buryja)
(Snoubenci libaji
staŕence ruce.)

La - ca, denk' mei - ner nicht im Bö - sen!
Ty, La - co, mne zle ne - vzpo - mí - nej!

Richter.
Rychtář.

Jetzt Ihr, Kü - ste - rin,
A včil, Ko - stel - nič - ko,

215

216

218

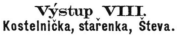

8. Szene.
Küsterin, die Alte, Stewa.

Výstup VIII.
Kostelnička, stařenka, Števa.

220

Küsterin.
Kostelnička.

Hal - tet mich,   ret - tet mich_
*Drž - te   mne,   braň - te   mne_*

Die Alte.
Stařenka.

Ach, was   sprichst   du,
A - le   dce   -   -   ro

222

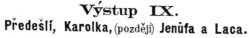

224

Selbst hab' ich's aus Bän-dern für mein
Sa - ma jsem ho ze svých pan - tlí

Kind ge-näht!__ **Richterin.**
po - pra - vi - la! **Rychtářka.**
Was
Ej

Mann, da hörst du es, daß sie da-von wis - sen!
Sly - šíš, rych - tá - ři! O - ni o tom vě - dí!

tut ihr,
li - dé,
wollt ihr's oh - ne Sarg be - gra - ben?
kte - rak jste ho do - pra - vi - li,

Tante.
Tetka.
Ru - he gebt ihm! Ru - he gebt ihm!
bez tru - hél - ky, bez vě - ně - čku!

Je - sus Ma - ri - a,
Je - ží - ši Kri - ste,
Je - sus Ma - ri - a,
Je - ží - ši Kri - ste,

228

234

236

238

Küsterin.
Kostelnička.

Rich - ter, nehmt mich nun, führt mich nun!...
Po - jdte, rych - tá - ři! *Veď - te mne!...*

Jenufa.
Jenůfa.

60

(Der **Richter** stützt die **Küsterin** und führt sie weg, die Menge drängt sich hinter ihnen hinaus.)
(Rychtář podepře Kostelničku v rameni a odchází. Za nimi se hrnou všichni.)

Tröst euch der Him - mel!
Pán - bůh vás po - těš!

p

ff

(Jenufa und Laca bleiben.)
(Zůstanou jen Jenůfa a Laca.)

longa

244

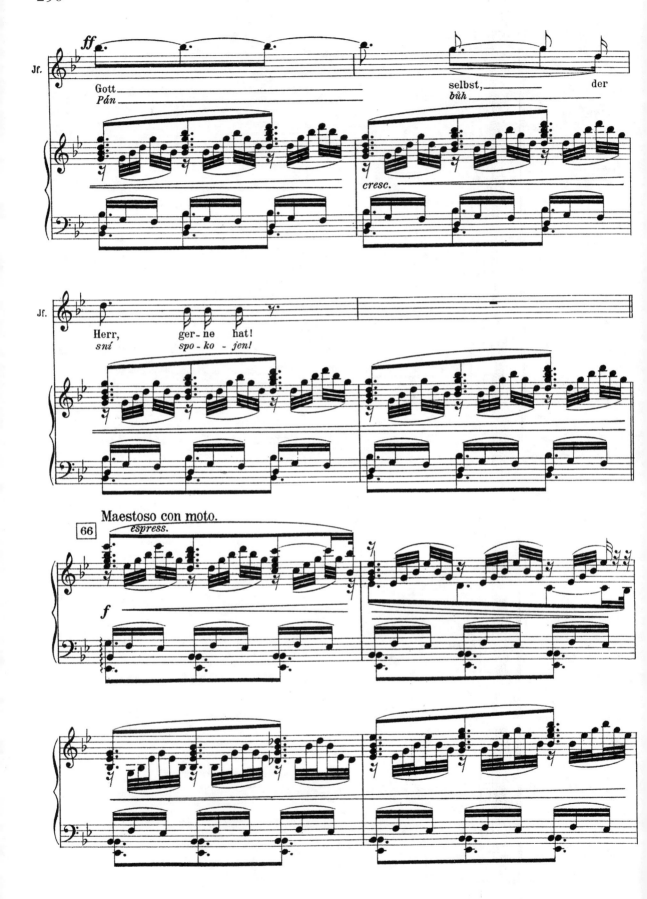

(Der Vorhang fällt.)
(Opona padá.)

Ende der Oper.
Konec Opery.